RUNWAYS TO RESILIENCE

The Art of Leading Beyond the Skies

NEHA ARORA

A Book By:
FOREVER SHININGS
Instagram - @forevershinings.co
forevershinings1@gmail.com

Book Title: Runways To Resilience: The Art of Leading Beyond the Skies

Book Author: Neha Arora

Published By: FOREVER SHININGS

First Edition: 2025

ISBN: 978-93-7406-083-4

About the Book

Ever tried calming a passenger convinced the plane is "definitely crashing" because of a little turbulence? Or explaining to someone that, no! their oversized bag will not magically shrink to fit the overhead bin?

Welcome to customer experience at 35,000 feet.

In Runways to Resilience, Neha Arora shares the hilarious, heartfelt, and sometimes downright ridiculous lessons she picked up in the skies and how they translate to leadership, business, and everyday life. From gate drama and meal meltdowns to startup turbulence and toddler negotiations, Neha proves that resilience is not about avoiding chaos. It's about navigating it with humour, grace, and maybe a well-timed extra dessert.

This is not another boring leadership manual. Think of it as your boarding pass to the messy, funny, and very human side of service and calm under pressure. You will laugh, nod, and maybe even rethink the way you handle your own "difficult passengers" whether they are clients, colleagues, bosses, or, let's be honest, family members.

Because here's the thing: leadership is not a title. It's an attitude. And sometimes the best lesson starts with a coffee, a smile, and the patience not to roll your eyes at 30,000 feet.

So, buckle up, this is your captain speaking: it's going to be a funny, bumpy, and surprisingly inspiring ride.

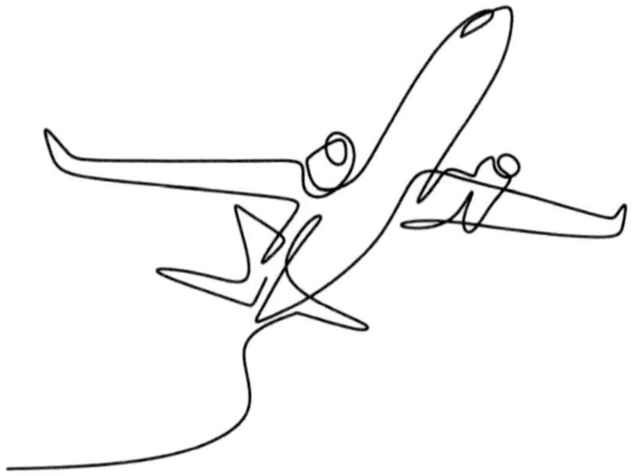

About the Author

Burgers, boarding passes, boardrooms- Neha's journey glides effortlessly through them all.

She began her journey at McDonald's, wearing a polo and cap that never quite fit, where she learned the art of patience when "fast food" never felt fast enough. Soon after, she joined British Airways as a travel advisor, helping passengers across time zones and discovering that sometimes the loudest voices only need the calmest replies.

From there, she traded counters and corporates for cabins, first with Vistara and later with Qatar Airways, where the world became her workplace.

Her passion for people and service led her to become a cabin crew instructor, guiding aspiring candidates and helping them successfully turn their dream of flying into reality. She then transitioned into the startup world as Vice President of Customer Experience, where she built customer-first strategies and cultures across the organization. Along the way, she embraced the most demanding role of all *-motherhood* - and later took off again as Chief Customer Strategy Officer at Eduroids, an ed-tech venture.

In *Runways to Resilience*, her debut book, Neha weaves humor, empathy, and insight into stories drawn from every stage of her journey. It's not just about the skies she has flown, but about the people, challenges, and resilience that connect them all.

Prologue
Before The Runway

My first uniform? Not glamorous at all. And no, not the school kind - I am talking about the first one I wore stepping into my career. No polished heels. No silk scarf.

No shiny airline wings. Just a McDonald's polo shirt and a cap that never quite agreed with my head.

That's where I learned the first rule of customer service: hungry people are negotiable, but *hangry* people? They are a whole different species. Hand them the wrong Coke and suddenly you are the villain in their personal soap opera. The trick? Be fast, be consistent, and smile, even when your legs are begging for a coffee break of their own.

But here's the thing, sometimes kindness showed up, quietly. I still remember one customer who asked for his burger without tomatoes. Somewhere between the rush of fries and fountain drinks, the tomato slipped through. I braced myself for a complaint. Instead, he just smiled, shrugged, and ate it without saying a word. No drama. No lecture. Just grace. That day I realized: patience can be as powerful as anger. And those are the customers you remember just as much as the loud ones.

From fries to flights, my next stop was Singapore Airlines, still not on the runways yet, just on the other side of the tarmac - boarding gates, arrival halls, delayed flights, and tearful passengers watching their connections disappear. I remember one businessman in a perfect grey suit paced like he was trading stocks with every step, muttering "unbelievable… just unbelievable," as if the delay was a personal attack on his portfolio.

But it wasn't always gloom. Some days looked straight out of a Bollywood film: families reuniting after years apart, honeymooners glowing like fairy lights, kids jumping around because it was their very first flight.

Here's what I realised: people don't always remember the delay or the chaos. They remember *how you treated them* when it all went wrong. A calm voice, a clear plan, and sometimes just looking them in the eye and saying, "I'll sort this out," could turn the whole scene around.

Then came British Airways, where I swapped boarding gates for a headset, yes, That's right, working as a travel advisor, speaking to passengers across time zones. Some were delightful. Some… let's just say the mute button became my emotional support system There was a man in New York whose voice was so loud it felt like it was bouncing off my headset into the next cubicle. Ten straight minutes of shouting about a missed flight, his tone sharp, his words clipped, like bullets over the line. I let him unload, fingers poised over my keyboard, waiting for the gap. And when it came, I said gently, *"I know this is stressful. Let me see what best I can do."*

His voice softened immediately, like someone had turned the volume dial down. By the end of the call, he was thanking me. Magic? Nope. Just empathy through a headset.

So, when I finally stepped onto an aircraft as cabin crew, I was not new to this game. I had lived it: from flipping burgers, to managing check-in chaos, to surviving angry callers. Cabin Crew was not the beginning of my customer experience journey. It was simply the next chapter.

And that's really what this book is about. The sky may have been my classroom, but the lessons are human ones: how you greet someone, how you recover when things go wrong, how you make people feel seen. These are not "airline" lessons. They are *life* lessons. They are leadership lessons.

Because leadership doesn't live in fancy theories or endless checklists. It lives in the basics: calm in turbulence, respect in the rush, presence when everyone else is distracted. Small things that people remember forever, whether you're at 35,000 feet or standing behind a counter with a cap that won't stay on straight.So, buckle up. This is not just a book about flying. It's about staying grounded when life throws turbulence your way.

Ladies and gentlemen, welcome aboard this book. Please fasten your seatbelts, keep your mind open, and prepare for take-off. Our cruising altitude will be equal parts humour, chaos, and leadership with a few complimentary snacks of wisdom along the way.

Index

WELCOME ABOARD

Chapter 1:
The First Greeting Matters

It was 3 a.m. at the airport, that strange time when your body is technically awake, but your spirit is still hitting snooze, your chai betrays you, and your body insists you should be asleep, but your uniform insists otherwise.

I stood at the aircraft door, uniform crisp, lipstick on, smile switched on like Wi-Fi. The kind of smile that says: *Yes, I haven't slept either, but let's pretend we are all thrilled to be here.*

Passengers moved down the aisle like kids dragged out of bed for school on a Monday morning. Hair sticking up in odd directions, hoodies zipped all the way up, some clutched travel pillows like lifejackets, some dragged half-asleep children, and most looked as if finding their seat number was the hardest math exam they had ever taken with the expressions that said, *"Why did I book this flight?"* The sound of seatbelts clicking was the closest thing to energy in the cabin

And then came Mr. Grumpy, Middle-aged. Salt-and-pepper hair that looked like it had wrestled with a pillow and lost. Shirt tucked in, tie hanging off his neck like it had given up on life. His cabin bag had one squeaky wheel that screamed louder than his sighs, and his face… oh, his face. Imagine someone who just got told their favourite biryani place had shut down forever.

That was Mr. Grumpy. Without so much as a glance, he shoved his boarding pass at me, sighed so heavily I thought he might pass out, and muttered something under his breath that sounded suspiciously like cursing the entire aviation industry. His whole aura screamed: *Do. Not. Engage.*

Now here is the thing about greetings. At that hour, I had two options. I could match his mood, robotic "welcome aboard," dead eyes, the kind of energy you forget before you've even sat down. Or I could flip it.

I chose mischief. I looked straight at him, smiled like I had all the energy in the world (lies), and said warmly:

"Welcome aboard, Mr. Gupta. Glad to have you with us."

He froze. Like someone had hit pause on his remote control. His eyes finally lifted, blinking as if he had just realized *oh, these flight attendants are actual humans, not robots*. And then, miracle of miracles, he smiled back. A real one. "Thank you," he said, but his eyes added, *"Wow, I really needed that."*

Fast forward a few hours, and there he was sipping tea, laughing with the crew, looking nothing like the storm cloud who had stomped on at 3 a.m. One tiny greeting had flipped his flight, and honestly, mine too.

Because the truth is, first greetings are not small talk. They are mood-setters. They decide if the flight is going to feel like one long bout of turbulence or if there's hope for smooth skies.

And trust me even at 3 a.m., when your patience is thinner than airplane coffee, that first "hello" is worth it.

Beyond The Runway

Picture your workplace on a Monday morning. The manager walks in looking like the weekend personally betrayed him and just like that, the whole team feels doomed. Then there is the colleague who mutters 'morning' without even looking up from their phone. You already know not to ask them for anything until lunch.

Now flip that. Imagine a person who walks in, makes eye contact, says your name, and greets you like they actually want you there. The energy in the room shifts instantly. One person's presence sets the tone for everyone else's day.

That's the leadership lesson. Greetings are not small talk. They are first impressions. They are mood-setters. Too many leaders wait for their teams to acknowledge them first, as if respect only flows one way. The best leaders know it starts with them.

A real leader does not just expect a greeting. They create it. They don't just acknowledge people; they make people feel acknowledged. They don't just walk in with authority; they walk in with presence.

Respect isn't owed because of your title. It's earned in the way you show up.

Chapter 2:
The Power Of The Uniform

When I first put on my cabin crew uniform, lipstick carefully applied, hair tied back so tight it could survive a hurricane.

I remember looking at myself in the mirror during training, makeup immaculate, uniform spotless. For a second, I barely recognized the girl staring back at me. She did not look nervous, underpaid, or exhausted. She looked… professional. In control. Ready to handle anything.

The funny part? That was the same effect it had on passengers.

The uniform does things. It straightens your back. It fixes your posture. It makes people listen to you in a way your normal clothes never will. I mean, I have walked into airports on my off days in jeans and sneakers and not one soul asked me anything. But put on that uniform and suddenly it's:

"Ma'am, is this the gate for London?"
"Excuse me, will this flight serve vegetarian meals?"
"Hi, can you tell me where the toilets are?"

And half the time, these were not even passengers for my airline. They just saw the outfit and assumed I had the answers to all of life's questions. (Spoiler: I didn't. I was usually just as lost as them.)

My favourite though? Once at Delhi Airport, a man actually came up to me at the terminal, looked me up and down, and said:

"Madam, can I take a picture with you?"

Like I was Anushka Sharma, I half expected him to ask for my autograph on his boarding pass though.

I remember a Doha–Singapore flight where a passenger wandered into the galley for a chat. He leaned casually against the galley shelf, sleeves rolled up, watch glinting under the cabin lights, and out of nowhere asked me about the **stock market**

The only thought running through my head was: *Sir, I can't tell you if Tesla will go up or down tomorrow. But I can tell you exactly where the emergency medical kit is, if the stock market crashes.*

That moment stuck with me, because it wasn't really about the stock market. It was about trust. Passengers ask you the strangest questions mid-flight, but beneath it all, what they are really looking for is reassurance. They want to believe you have got things under control, even if it's far outside your job description.

The moment we walked through the boarding gate, passengers transformed. Kids suddenly looked at us like superheroes. Tired business travellers who had been screaming into their phones softened their tone. Even the most nervous flyer seemed to breathe easier. Why? Because the uniform whispered one thing: *"Relax. We have got this."*

What passengers didn't know was that sometimes under that uniform, I was exhausted, hungry, or quietly praying the turbulence wouldn't be too rough. But the uniform worked like armor. Even if I didn't feel calm, the moment I looked in the mirror, I *looked* calm. And strangely, that made me act calm too.

A passenger once told me, "You all look so put together. It makes me feel safe." I smiled, but inside I laughed. Safe? My toes were numb in those shoes, and my hair bun was holding on for dear life. But he was right. The uniform was not just about grooming; it was about presence.

Beyond The Runway

Presence is power. People notice how you show up before you say a single word. The way you stand, dress, or carry yourself tells them whether to trust you, ignore you, or doubt you.

For me, the uniform was never just fabric. It was a signal.

A promise of professionalism to passengers. And on tough days, it was also a quiet reminder to myself: *You are capable. You are in control. You can do this.*

In leadership, the uniform may not be navy and gold, but it exists all the same. Sometimes it's a sharp suit in the boardroom. Sometimes it's the calm voice on a stressful call. Sometimes it's simply showing up to a Zoom with focus instead of distraction. However, it looks, presence sets the tone.

The power of the uniform isn't lipstick or heels. It's the switch it flips inside you, the voice that says: *I'm ready. People are watching. Time to deliver.*

Because the truth is, leadership does not start when you open your mouth. It starts the moment you walk in.

Chapter 3:
Coffee Or Champagne?

In business class, the real game isn't about what's in the glass. It's about how you *offer* it.

Forget the ads where a smiling crew member floats down the aisle with a silver tray and a perfect "Coffee or champagne?" That's not how it works. In reality, the script is softer, more open: *"Welcome on board. May I offer you something to drink before take-off? We have champagne, fresh juices, soft drinks, or coffee if you would prefer."* The words matter less than the way you lean in, the tone you use, the moment you make them feel like they are not just another seat number.

Now picture this.

Row 2A. He is already buckled in before half the cabin has boarded. Jacket folded with military precision, laptop open, eyes flicking between screens like he is running Wall Street from seat 2A. When I ask, "May I offer you something to drink?" he doesn't even look up. "Coffee, please." Just that. No eye contact, no smile. Five minutes later, when I set the cup down exactly the way he wants it, he exhales- a long, heavy sigh, the kind that says, *finally, something in my day is under control.* In that moment, it was not coffee. It was oxygen.

Row 3D is a whole different movie. Newlyweds on their honeymoon. Obvious, because their sneakers match and they haven't stopped holding hands since the gate(except they told me as soon they got on the plane). They are glowing like fairy lights strung across the aisle. Same question: "What may I offer you?" Their eyes meet, then mine. "Champagne!" And just like that, the cabin shifts, suddenly it's not a flight, it's the start of their honeymoon party at 35,000 feet.

That's the thing: you never assume. You ask. But over time, you develop a radar. A sixth sense. The ones with serious faces, navy suits, and thumbs flying over their phones? Coffee. The ones who play with the seat controls like they just discovered a spaceship? Champagne.
And then… the curveballs.

The CEO in a three-piece suit, face carved from stone, watch worth more than my car. At 9 a.m., he does not want coffee. He wants champagne -cold, sparkling, unapologetic. Suddenly, he is grinning like a kid ditching school, and I am reminded that even CEOs need bubbles sometimes.

Or the honeymoon couple, glowing like they swallowed the sun, who lower their voices and whisper, "Actually… coffee." As if caffeine is the secret glue that will hold their love story together better than champagne ever could.

That's the magic. It was never about what's poured. Nobody remembers if it was Brut or Arabica. They remember the moment. The pause. The smile.

The way they felt seen, understood, and just for a second like the entire cabin existed only for them.

Because in the end, service is not about drinks. It's about reading people. And it's about asking the question in the first place.

Beyond The Runway

Personalization isn't just good service, it's good leadership.

In business, just like on a plane, people have their own version of "coffee or champagne."

Some employees crave caffeine: focus, clarity, structure. They want deadlines, bullet points, and action plans. Others want bubbles: celebration, recognition, energy.

They light up with encouragement, team shoutouts, and the occasional "you nailed it."

The problem? Too many leaders assume everyone drinks from the same glass. They hand out coffee to the bubbly ones, champagne to the caffeine crew, and then wonder why nobody looks satisfied.

The real secret isn't guessing. It is asking. It is noticing the difference between someone who just survived a brutal week and someone who needs their win acknowledged. One wants fuel, the other wants fizz.

Leadership isn't about pouring the same thing for everyone. It is about knowing when your people need energy, when they need celebration, and serving it with a smile.And no, spiking the coffee with champagne is not leadership. That is just brunch.

Chapter 4:
Gate Drama And Happy Tears

Airports are not quiet places. They are emotional playgrounds where you can see every shade of human mood in a single hour.

At the gate, I have seen passengers running like they were auditioning for the Olympics -briefcases flapping, laptop bags banging against their hips, and expressions so desperate you'd think the plane was leaving without them personally, even though 200 others were calmly seated.

I have seen families in full-blown passport drama. The father clutching boarding passes like they were state secrets, the mother snapping, *"I told you to keep them in your bag,"* while the teenage son rolls his eyes so hard you worry, they might get stuck. Passports and tempers flying at the same time- it's like live theatre, only without an interval.

And of course, there are the latecomers. The ones who walk up to the gate in slow motion, as if they are starring in their own movie, only to gasp in horror when told, "Boarding closed 20 minutes ago." Their eyes widen, mouths drop, and they stare at the gate agent like this is breaking news just flashed on CNN. Honestly, ground staff deserve medals- Olympic gold, at the very least.

But here's the flip side: for every meltdown, there's a moment that melts your heart.

A grandmother clutching a bunch of slightly crumpled marigolds, her saree pleats uneven from rushing, tears streaming down her cheeks as she spots her grandchild for the very first time. Her hands tremble as she reaches out, half laughing, half crying, as if years of waiting suddenly collapsed into one hug.

A couple grinning ear to ear, the kind of smile that makes everyone else around them smile too. She is in a bright new kurta, red bangles jingling as she tugs at his arm; he is in jeans and a crisp shirt, holding their passports like they are golden tickets. Whispering about their honeymoon like it's a secret, they lean so close you wonder if they even realize anyone else is watching.

And then the kids -oh, the kids. Shoes flashing neon lights with every step, cartoon backpacks bouncing against their tiny shoulders, some riding on their trunkies, eyes as wide as the departure board. They hop around the gate area like wind-up toys, pointing at planes outside the window and squealing, "Is that OURS?"

That's the magic of airports. On one side of the terminal, someone is swearing at the departure board. On the other side, someone is hugging like they have just won the lottery. And in the middle of it all is you- the one in uniform, trying to hold everything together with a calm voice and a half-decent smile.

The trick I learned? You can't control the emotions people walk in with. But you *can* control the emotion they walk away with. Sometimes it's explaining a gate change without sounding like a robot. Sometimes it's sharing in the joy of a reunion, even if the hug is not yours.

Gate drama and happy tears will always exist side by side.

Your job is simple: manage the first, celebrate the second.

Customer experience isn't just about solving problems. It's about holding space for the chaos and the joy at the same time.

Beyond The Runway

Every workplace has its own version of gate drama and happy tears.

At one desk, someone is fuming because the project deadline feels impossible. Two seats away, another person is grinning because their idea just got approved. In one corner, there's frustration. In the other, celebration.

Same office, same day, completely different moods.

That's what leadership really is: holding space for both at once. You don't get to choose only the cheerful moments. You have to steady the drama without letting it spill over, and still celebrate the joy without letting it get lost.

Because people rarely remember the technical details of what you said or did. They remember how you made them feel when they were at their most stressed, or their most excited. Calm the storm. Share the sunshine. That balance is what earns trust.

Chapter 5:
Turbulence Inside And Out

The seatbelt sign pinged. The cabin lights flickered. A half-full coffee decided to leap off the tray and land in someone's lap. Welcome to turbulence - the rollercoaster ride nobody actually asked for.

Here's the thing about turbulence: passengers don't look at the captain -of course not, because he is locked behind a door and, frankly, seeing him in the cabin at the that time would only freak them out more. They don't grab the safety manual. They look at us. The cabin crew standing in the aisle, holding the trolley, trying not to fall over in heels while pretending this is completely normal.

I still remember my first real turbulence. My stomach dropped faster than the plane did. Every instinct screamed panic. But my training whispered, *breathe, steady, smile.* So, I smiled, braced myself, and said calmly, "Ladies and gentlemen, please remain seated with your seatbelts fastened."

Inside, I was thinking: *If this gets worse, I am joining you in those seatbelts.* Outside, I looked calm. And the funny thing? The passengers copied me. A nervous flyer, a woman in her forties with perfectly blow-dried hair and a handbag clutched like it was a ration card in the 90s, finally loosened her white-knuckle grip on the armrest.

She glanced at me, saw my calm smile, and exhaled like she had been holding her breath since take-off.

Two rows back, a little boy in a bright red Spiderman T-shirt threw his hands in the air and squealed like we had just taken him on the world's coolest rollercoaster.

And then there was the poor man with coffee in his lap. Middle-aged, office-ready shirt now looking like it belonged in an abstract art gallery. He blinked at me, gave a little laugh, and shrugged as if to say, *"Well, at least it's not red wine."*

That day, I realised turbulence is not just about bumps in the sky. It's about how people react to them. If the crew panics, everyone panics. If the crew looks calm, passengers feel safe. Calm is contagious.

Beyond The Runway

Turbulence does not just shake airplanes. It shakes workplaces too..

In work, in service, in leadership, chaos will show up uninvited.

In retail, it's the customer yelling because the sale price didn't ring up at checkout.

In tech, it's the app crashing five minutes before a big demo.

In hospitality, it's the wedding party whose flowers don't arrive on time.

In project teams, it's the last-minute client change that throws months of work off track.

In leadership, it's the surprise resignation, the budget cut, or the crisis that arrives just as you thought things were smooth..

The bumps are inevitable. But the reaction? That's optional. If a leader radiates panic, the entire team spirals. If a leader projects calm, people anchor to it.That's why real leadership is not about avoiding turbulence. It's about managing the emotions around it, showing steadiness when everything else is shaking, and reminding people that they can get through the ride.

Chapter 6:
The Difficult Passenger Club

Every flight has at least one. The passenger who thinks rules don't apply to them. The one who presses the call bell like it's a video game button. The one who insists their bag will fit in the overhead bin (physics says no, but they are convinced otherwise).

I once had a passenger who demanded an upgrade mid-air. Not before boarding. Not at the gate. **Mid-flight**, when every seat was already full. He was in his late fifties, hair slicked back with more gel than gravity could handle, silver watch flashing every time he waved his hand for emphasis. He leaned in, lowered his voice like he was sharing a state secret, and said with complete seriousness: "Make it happen."

I smiled politely and explained the reality. His reaction? He sighed so loudly I thought he was trying to power the aircraft with his lungs. He shifted in his seat, tapped his fingers on the armrest, and groaned dramatically every few minutes as if to remind the world of his suffering. For the next hour, it was like flying with a one-man opera.

And then there was *the meal guy.* Mid-forties, business suit that had clearly seen better days, tie pulled loose as though he had already fought three battles that week. He was the kind of man who spoke in declarations, not conversations.

When I explained that his preferred meal was finished, He actually asked, "Do you know who I am?" I mean, If you have to ask that question, you have already lost the plot.

The trick with difficult passengers is not to "win." It's to de-escalate without losing your own dignity. Stay calm, stay polite, and set boundaries. Smile, but not so much that it looks like you are inviting more drama. Sometimes it's about offering alternatives, sometimes it's about standing firm. Always, it's about remembering their mood does not get to decide yours.

Beyond The Runway

Every workplace has its own "difficult passengers."

In hospitality, it's the guest who wants a suite for the price of a standard room.

In corporate life, it's the client who demands rewrites at midnight after approving everything the night before.

In teams, it's the colleague who hits "reply all" like it's their personal call bell.

But here's the truth: the real test of leadership isn't how you manage the easy ones. It's how you deal with the impossible ones without letting them drain your energy or dictate your tone. You don't have to "win" the drama.

You have to de-escalate it, set boundaries, and keep your dignity intact.

And sometimes, let's be brutally honest- it's the leader who is the difficult passenger. The boss who shuts down ideas before hearing them. The manager who treats people like projects instead of humans. If every meeting feels like a standoff, maybe the turbulence isn't the team—it's you.

Great leaders have the courage to admit when they have become the problem. They pause. They listen. They reset the tone. Because respect doesn't trickle down, it starts at the top.

The best leaders do not fight to be the smartest in the room or the loudest at the table. They notice the quiet thinker with the sharp idea. They encourage the junior who just needs a nudge. They trust the team member who shines brightest when given space.

True leadership isn't about flashing your own superpowers. It's about helping others discover theirs.

And in the end, leadership isn't about matching moods. It's about modelling the one you want the room to follow.

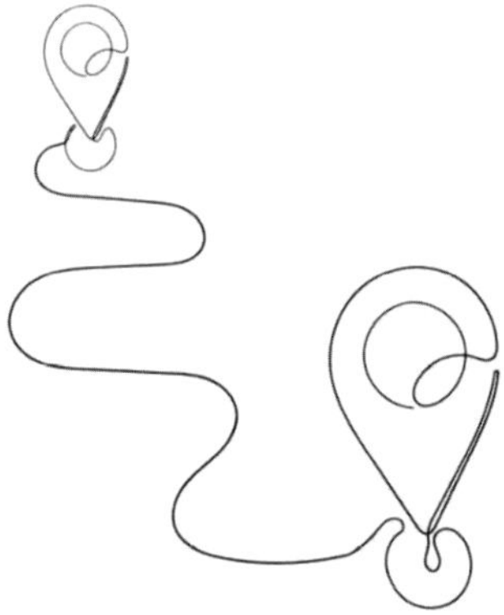

Chapter 7: Not All Turbulence Comes From The Sky

Passengers are not always the hardest part of the job. Sometimes, it's the people in your own uniform. Managers. The ones who should be guiding the ship but occasionally act like they have mistaken the aisle for a runway.

It was a red-eye to London, never part of my roster. I got yanked from standby to fill in for another crew member and trust me, the lucky one wasn't me, it was the person who got to stay home in pyjamas while I dragged mine onto the aircraft.

The mood was set right from the briefing room. That's where **Mr. Nitpick** made his entrance. Clipboard tucked under his arm, posture straight as a ruler, he began the pre-flight checks with the enthusiasm of someone grading a math exam. "Ladies, gentlemen, let's keep the standards tight tonight," he announced, tapping his pen like a judge with a gavel. His eyes scanned us one by one-hair neat, scarves aligned, nails inspected, pausing just long enough to make you wonder if you would accidentally smuggled contraband eyeliner onboard.

When he got to the galley preparations, the sermon began.

"Remember," he said, wagging a finger, "glasses must be aligned. Not approximately aligned. Perfectly aligned.

The passenger may not notice, but I will."

I exchanged a look with my colleague across the table- the kind of look that says, *brace yourself, this is going to be a long night.*

Fast forward a few hours. The cabin lights were dim, passengers sinking into their blankets, and the galley was finally quiet enough for us to breathe. That's when I heard it- the sharp rhythm of shoes clicking down the aisle…

He approached with the seriousness of a surgeon about to perform open-heart surgery. Eyes scanning, lips pursed, clipboard clutched like it held the secrets of the universe.

He stopped at the galley, leaned in, and frowned.

"These glasses," he said, pointing to the perfectly neat champagne flutes, "are not aligned to standard."

I glanced at the tray. Twelve sparkling glasses. Perfect to any normal eye. But apparently not to his sacred millimetre scale. We rearranged them while he watched like an art critic judging the Mona Lisa. Finally, after a long pause, He gave a serious nod, as if our tray had just saved the aircraft from emergency landing.

Passengers in row 5 looked over, probably wondering if misaligned glasses had caused the last turbulence. I wanted to laugh but instead I smiled, "Of course." Because sometimes, you let the Captain Nitpicks win their little wars so you can win the real battles- keeping passengers happy.

And then there were the managers who were not obsessed with objects but with people- specifically, with timing them. One supervisor, whom we nicknamed The Stopwatch, had a strange hobby. He timed bathroom breaks. Yes, with a watch. I came back from one and he whispered, "Three minutes, forty seconds. Too long."

Too long for what? A Guinness World Record? I almost asked if he wanted a demonstration of faster techniques, but I bit my tongue, nodded, and said, "Noted." Because sometimes, rolling your eyes in your head is the only way to survive.

But the one who tested me the most wasn't Captain Nitpick or The Stopwatch. It was a ground supervisor during a storm in Mumbai. Flights were delayed, families crying, honeymooners panicking, passengers shouting over each other. The terminal was chaos. And there he was, pacing with a frown so deep it could have been carved in stone. His contribution? Repeating, "This is unacceptable," over and over, as if the monsoon would stop out of respect.

Meanwhile, my team stood frozen, waiting. So, I smiled, clapped my hands, and said, "Alright, let's split the load. Priya, take the passengers with missed connections.

Rahul, handle wheelchairs, and special assistance. I will deal with the loud ones. Within minutes, order began to return. The businessman who was yelling finally had an alternate flight. The stranded family got a hotel room. The wheelchair passenger was on his way to assistance. By the time our supervisor returned from "assessing the situation," everything was under control. He nodded like he had fixed it himself. We let him take the credit, because in that moment, leadership was not about titles. It was about stepping up when the person with the title did not.

And that's the truth about turbulence from managers. Sometimes it looks like glasses being shifted by millimetres. Sometimes it looks like a stopwatch hovering outside the bathroom door. And sometimes, it's the silence of the person who should have been leading. But every one of them taught me something: what not to do. And in their own way, they forced me to grow steadier, calmer, and braver.

Because the real test of leadership isn't how straight your glasses are or how fast your team can pee. It's how steady you stay when everyone else is panicking. And that lesson-well, that one carries far beyond the runway.

Beyond The Runway- For Leaders

Stop nitpicking, start leading.

People do not follow you because you line up glasses perfectly or point out every tiny mistake. They follow you when you give them confidence and direction. A nitpicking boss makes people nervous. A guiding boss makes people stronger.

Do not go silent when things go wrong.

A quiet boss in a crisis is scarier than the crisis itself. If your team is panicking, say something. Even if it's simple like, *"We'll figure this out together."* People feel calmer when they know someone is steering the ship.

Show up, do not hide.

Your team does not need you to be perfect. They need you to be present. Stand with them. Speak to them. Be visible. A leader who disappears when things get messy loses trust fast.

Use words to calm, not confuse.

In a flight, one clear announcement from the captain *"It's turbulence, it will pass"* can settle 300 nervous passengers. Leaders work the same way. Say things clearly. Give direction. Confusion is heavier than bad news.

Your mood spreads faster than Wi-Fi.

If you are angry, sarcastic, or stressed, your team will catch it instantly. But if you stay steady, calm, and positive, they will mirror that too. Your energy is the weather inside the room.

Trust your people to rise.

Do not hover. Do not micromanage. Let people step up. Often, the best ideas or solutions come when the leader simply says, *"I trust you-handle it."* People want to feel capable, not controlled.

See the human, not just the uniform.

Behind every employee is a person- tired, hopeful, maybe stressed about life outside work. A quick "Good job" or "Thanks for handling that" can lift someone more than you realize. Recognition builds loyalty faster than rules ever will.

The Big Lesson

Leadership isn't about looking perfect in calm times. It's about how steady you stay when everything shakes. People won't remember the rules you enforced. They'll remember if you made them feel safe, capable, and supported when it mattered most.

Beyond The Runway: For Team Members

Choose your battles wisely.

Not every nitpick deserves your energy. Sometimes nodding and moving on is the smartest survival tool.

Step up when leadership steps back.

A crisis can be your chance to lead from wherever you stand. Influence is not about title - it's about action.

Empathy goes both ways.

Even the clipboard-holder has pressures you may not see. You don't have to agree with them, but understanding that weight helps you carry yours without resentment.

Stay professional, not personal.

A bad mood, a harsh word, or nitpicking instructions, do not take it home with you. Protect your peace. Their stress doesn't have to become your stress.

Support your teammates.

When a manager piles pressure on one person, step in and help. A strong team can make even a weak leader look better, and you will earn loyalty from your peers.

Use humour as a shield.

A shared eye-roll or a quiet joke in the galley can defuse tension and remind you that you are not alone. Laughter is a survival tool.

Know when to speak up.

There is a difference between compliance and silence. If something affects safety, fairness, or dignity, use your voice- calmly but firmly.

Turn frustration into fuel.

Every difficult manager is teaching you how *not* to lead. File away the lesson. One day when you're in charge, you'll know exactly what to do differently.

The Big Lesson

You cannot control who manages you, but you can always control how you respond. Every tough shift is training - not just in patience, but in leadership you will carry into your own future

Chapter 8:
Brace For Impact?

Feedback is like turbulence. Done right, it shakes you just enough to stay alert. Done wrong, it rattles your confidence so badly you just want to grab an oxygen mask.

I first saw this during my time at British Airways, long before I ever put on a cabin crew uniform.

There I was, wearing a headset in a call center cubicle, speaking to passengers across time zones. One day I handled a furious caller from New York. His voice was so loud the entire floor could probably hear him without their headsets. Ten minutes of nonstop shouting about a missed connection.

I stayed calm, let him vent, and when the gap finally came, I said gently: “I know this is stressful. Let me see what I can do.”

It worked. His tone softened. By the end, he was thanking me.

I took off my headset, feeling a little proud. That’s when *Mr. Script* swooped in. Our floor manager, who believed feedback was best given immediately and preferably without any cushioning.

"You did not use the exact phrase *'We sincerely apologise for the inconvenience'*. Stick to the script next time."

That was it. No recognition for calming an angry passenger. No acknowledgment of empathy. Just a ding for not quoting the airline manual word-for-word.

It struck me then, the person I served gave me encouragement, the person I reported to gave me a lecture. That's when I realised, bad feedback doesn't just deflate people. It trains them to stop trusting their instincts. It encourages box-ticking instead of real impact.

Years later, in Doha, I saw the same thing unfold in the skies.

We were in the briefing room at 2 a.m., uniforms crisp, hair buns tight, the kind of silence where everyone pretends to be wide awake. The supervisor walked in, scanned the room, and went straight for Priya, a brand-new crew member.

"Your smile," she said, "is too much. Too wide. Looks fake."

The room fell silent. Priya's smile slipped instantly. One sentence, delivered at the wrong time in the wrong way, drained the light out of her.

The irony? A passenger on that flight later wrote a compliment card about Priya's "warm and welcoming smile." The very thing criticized was the thing most valued.

But not all feedback was turbulence. Some leaders knew how to steady you mid-flight.

At Qatar Airways, after one particularly chaotic sector, our purser pulled me aside in the galley. It had been one of those flights where nothing seemed to go smoothly, last-minute special meals, a passenger fainting mid-service, turbulence shaking the trays. I was convinced I had failed at keeping things under control.

Instead of a public critique, she quietly said:

"You handled yourself well. You stayed calm, and that calmed the passengers. Next time, just remember to delegate earlier - you don't need to carry it all yourself."

That was it. One line that acknowledged what I had done right and gave me one clear way to improve. I walked away taller, not smaller. Encouraged, not embarrassed.

And when I eventually stepped into leadership myself, I knew exactly whose traits to carry forward. Not the manager who nitpicked scripts. Not the supervisor who dimmed a junior's smile. But the leader who gave feedback like a steadying hand in turbulence firm enough to guide, gentle enough to lift.

Beyond The Runway

The truth is, feedback is not meant to send people into *brace position.* It's meant to help them keep flying.
The difference between feedback that lifts and feedback that crushes often comes down to how it's given:

When you say it matters. Correct in private, celebrate in public.

How you say it matters. Feedback should feel like guidance, not a gavel.

What you focus on matters. The bigger picture is more important than a crooked smile or a missed word.

Mistakes happen. They are not failures - they are practice.
The right feedback helps people bounce back stronger.
People will not remember every detail of your feedback.

But they will remember whether you left them bracing for impact or steady enough to soar.

Because leadership is not about catching people when they stumble. It's about giving them wings strong enough to rise again.

Chapter 9:
When ~~Things~~ Wings Go Wrong

Airlines make schedules. The universe makes jokes. Meals run out, bags go missing, delays stretch for hours, and sometimes an entire entertainment system decides to take the day off.

I once worked a flight where two passengers wanted the *last chicken meal.* One was a middle-aged man in a polo shirt, leaning back with the confidence of someone who believed chicken was his birthright. The other, a younger guy in noise-cancelling headphones, was already clutching his tray like he had just won it in Olympics.
When I told Mr. Polo that the chicken was gone, he looked at me like I'd personally sabotaged his dinner plans. His glare said, *"This is a betrayal."* Meanwhile, Mr. Headphones was guarding that tray like it was the Kohinoor diamond. I stood there, stuck in what I now call *poultry politics.*

In the end, I offered Mr. Polo the alternative meal, upgraded with an extra dessert and my most persuasive smile- the one that says *"trust me, this tastes just as good, and no, you won't die without chicken."* He ate it. He even thanked me later. Crisis averted.

Then there was the bag incident. A sharply dressed man in his thirties arrived at the carousel, clearly dressed for holiday mode, crisp white linen shirt, sleeves rolled just so, pastel shorts, and sunglasses perched on his head like a crown. He looked like an Instagram ad for *"escape to the Maldives."* Except his suitcase had decided to take its own vacation in another city. The moment he realised, his face went redder than a delayed departure board. He was furious, of course, and it was not even my department. But in that moment, he did not care about departments. He cared that someone listened to him. So, I acknowledged his frustration, apologised, and calmly directed him to the right counter where baggage claims were handled.

He was not exactly cheerful, but he walked away less angry because sometimes people don't need you to solve the whole problem, they just need you to guide them without brushing them off.

That's the thing about when things go wrong: people don't need perfection. They need recovery. They need to feel that someone is on their side, even if all you are doing is pointing them in the right direction.

Beyond The Runway

Every job has its "missing baggage" moments.
In **restaurants**, it's when the kitchen runs out of the dish a customer came for.

In **tech**, it's when a big update crashes right in front of a client demo.

In **offices**, the big presentation crashes five minutes before it's due

In **leadership**, it's when a project derails and the team looks to you for direction.

Here's the thing: people do not expect flawlessness. What they do expect is that when things break, you do not brush them off. You acknowledge the problem, point them to the right next step, and make them feel cared for in the process.

That's the real test of leadership. Not in the easy moments when everything runs on time, but in the messy ones when the plan falls apart. The strongest leaders do not deflect or blame. They steady the room, take responsibility, and turn chaos into clarity.

Trust is never built by perfection. It's built in recovery. It's built in the way you show up when things go wrong.

Calm voices. Honest words. Small gestures that say, *I have got you.*

The best leaders, like the best crew, are not remembered for avoiding turbulence. They are remembered for helping people land through it

.

Chapter 10:
Cultures In The Cabin

One of the best things about flying was that the cabin felt like a mini United Nations at 35,000 feet. In a single aisle, you could serve twenty nationalities, twenty accents, and twenty different definitions of "good service."

I once served an Italian gentleman who waved his hand for attention like he was hailing a taxi in Rome. Loud, direct, unapologetic- for him, volume was just energy, not rudeness. Two rows later, a Japanese passenger raised one finger ever so politely, barely above shoulder level, so subtle I almost missed it. For him, quiet signals were respectful; loud demands would have felt impolite.

In the same flight, an American passenger smiled broadly, called me by name (after sneakily reading my badge), and immediately asked, "So what's good today, Neha?" - chatty, friendly, expecting warmth. Meanwhile, a German passenger gave me his order like a checklist: "Still water.

No ice. Thank you." Clear, efficient, no small talk. Not cold, just precise.

And it wasn't just the passengers. Behind the galley curtain, every flight was its own cultural cocktail. We almost never had the same crew twice.

One day I would be paired with a Spanish colleague who believed service should be quick, lively, and full of gestures- trays flying out with cheerful speed. The next day, a Korean colleague who approached every service like choreography: precise steps, exact placement, everything flawless. Then a South African colleague who cracked jokes at every turn, putting passengers at ease with humor before they even asked for anything.

Each brought their own rhythm, their own habits, their own way of defining “professional.” And the fun part? you weren’t just adapting to passengers, you were adapting to your team too and you had to do it fast, because the doors were armed and cross-checked.

That was the real lesson: service doesn’t mean the same thing to everyone. But respect does. The trick was learning to adapt without losing yourself. To read signals, not just faces. To adjust tone and pace without faking who you were.

Because when the cabin became a mini United Nations, the goal was not to be the same for everyone. The goal was to make everyone feel seen in their own language of respect.

Beyond The Runway

Everyday life is multicultural too. Dinner with in-laws feels like its own cross-cultural negotiation. A group of friends may interpret the same silence in different ways.

Misunderstandings are not always about bad intent sometimes they are about different playbooks.

Every workplace today is its own mini United Nations.

You may not be serving meals at 35,000 feet, but you are definitely working with people who define "respect" differently.

In tech, your American colleague may love brainstorming out loud, while your Japanese colleague prefers to think quietly and share ideas once they're polished.

In finance, a German client may want a detailed, structured proposal, while a Brazilian client expects warmth, flexibility, and plenty of personal rapport.

Similarly, Hospitality isn't one-size-fits-all: Brits may find check-ins intrusive, Indians may find silence neglectful..

The leadership lesson? Service, teamwork, and management are not "one-size-fits-all." Great leaders adapt- they adjust tone, pace, and style depending on who is in front of them. But they don't lose themselves in the process.

Because whether it's passengers or employees, people don't always agree on what good service looks like. But they always recognize when they're treated with respect. The cabin taught me this: cultures may differ, but kindness translates everywhere.

Chapter 11: Luxury Beyond The Seat

Ask anyone what luxury on a flight looks like and they will say: champagne, lie-flat beds, caviar, maybe a golden ticket to silence crying babies. But when you have served in premium cabins, you learn quickly that luxury doesn't always come wrapped in a glass of Dom Pérignon.

I once had a passenger in business class who looked completely drained. Mid-thirties, still in a suit but with the tie already loosened, his eyes heavy with the kind of fatigue only back-to-back meetings can create. He didn't want champagne. He didn't even want dinner. He leaned in, voice barely above a whisper:

"Could I just have my bed made quickly? I really need to sleep."

So we skipped the service, tucked him in with an extra blanket, and dimmed the lights around him. By morning, he thanked me like I had given him a week-long holiday. Another time, an elderly lady pressed the call bell. She was petite, with silver hair pinned neatly, and pearls still in her ears- the kind of woman who looked like she had once run a household with military precision. She held out a small pill bottle with shaky hands and asked, almost apologetically, if I could help her open it.

That was her “luxury” moment: not champagne, not caviar, just someone treating her with patience, not rushing her like she was an inconvenience. When I handed it back, her smile was warmer than any passenger whose glass I’d topped up with vintage champagne.

And then there was the man who simply wanted conversation. Polo shirt, wedding ring shining as he fiddled with his watch. He didn’t want to network or brag. He just needed to talk about missing his daughter back home. For ten quiet minutes, I listened while he showed me her photo and told me how proud he was of her. That flight, the luxury wasn’t the seat or the menu. It was the fact that someone gave him undistracted human attention. That’s when I realised: the seat, the food, the perks - they are just props. Luxury is in the way you notice someone’s *real* need, even if it is as small as sleep, help, or human connection.

Beyond The Runway

Luxury is not always caviar and champagne - outside the cabin, it looks different too.

In an office, luxury might be a manager who actually ends a meeting on time so people can breathe.

For a team member, luxury might be a boss who listens without checking their phone.

In customer service, luxury might be a rep who says, “I’ll handle this for you,” instead of bouncing you around departments.

In **leadership**, it’s never about beanbags in the office or flashy perks but a manager who gives you time, respect, and space when you need it.

The lesson? Real luxury is about presence. It’s about noticing what someone *really* needs in that moment and delivering it with respect. Titles and benefits might impress people for a while, but genuine attention and empathy are what make them stay.

Chapter 12: Technology With A Human Touch

Airlines love their systems. We had portals, codes, endless screens of data. Sabre looked like "The Matrix" for travel nerds. Flight information updated every second, bags were tagged with more accuracy than some people's birthdays, and meal counts were tracked like military operations.

But here's the catch: none of it mattered if the human piece was missing.

I once had a passenger whose boarding pass didn't scan.

He was in his early forties, T-shirt tucked in too tightly, briefcase clutched to his chest as if it held state secrets.

His ears turned pink, his eyes flicked nervously to the line of passengers behind him, and in that moment, he looked less like a business traveller and more like a kid about to be scolded in school.

The machine beeped red. Error.

I smiled and said, "Don't worry, happens all the time." With a quick manual check, the green light appeared and he finally exhaled. His shoulders dropped, his grip on the briefcase loosened, and he walked on with his dignity intact.

Sometimes the computer says error. The human response is what makes all the difference.

Another time, the system proudly displayed *"Vegetarian Meal: Loaded."* Except… the galley trays told a different story. And the passenger? She was maybe late twenties, hair tied in a messy bun, oversized hoodie that screamed "comfort first," glasses sliding down her nose as she sat reading a thick paperback. She looked up at me, tilted her head, and said with a half-smile, "So… no veg meal?

What's the plan then?" Her tone was not angry, just hungry - and you don't mess with hungry. No app could fix that moment. What did? An honest apology, a swap with some salad, I prepared like the *Master chef* onboard, plus an extra dessert delivered with my *"trust me, this is better than chicken"* smile.

That's the thing about technology: Technology is brilliant at tasks, but not at feelings. It can scan a bag, but not reassure the traveller who lost it. It can assign a seat, but not make the person feel welcome in it. That's where humans still matter. Tech keeps planes flying. People keep passengers human.

Beyond The Runway

Technology is great… until it throws a tantrum. And it always picks the worst moment.

In offices, it's the Zoom call that freezes right when your boss asks for your opinion.

In retail, it's the billing system that crashes on Black Friday while customers form a queue longer than a runway.

In customer service, it's the chatbot that proudly says *"How can I help?"* but can't answer a single real question.

And in finance, it's that "flawless" Excel sheet that suddenly refuses to open five minutes before the client presentation.

The pattern is always the same: the system fails, people panic and someone human has to step in. A calm laugh, a quick workaround, even a simple *"Don't worry, we'll fix this"* is worth more than all the fancy software in the world.

That is where leadership comes in. Tools can schedule tasks, but they can't inspire action. Dashboards can track performance, but they can't lift morale when things fall apart. No software update has ever restored trust but a steady leader can.

The truth is, people rarely remember the tool that worked.

They remember the leader who stayed present when everything else didn't.

Technology keeps you efficient. Leadership keeps you human. And you need both for the journey to work.
And let's be honest: no matter how advanced AI gets, people will always prefer a leader who actually remembers their name.

Chapter 13: Gateways, Not Goodbyes

When I finally got my wings, I also had to hand in my corporate ID card. Before stepping into the skies, I was working a regular corporate job, complete with endless emails, coffee breaks, and meetings that could have been just emails. Resigning from that world felt like my first mini takeoff, a leap from desk to cabin, excel sheets to safety demos.

I thought it would be simple. Pass on the papers. Smile through a farewell cake. Maybe even get a nice card with too many signatures squeezed onto it. A clean departure. But here's what I didn't expect. The moment my resignation email went out, the atmosphere shifted faster than an aircraft hitting decompression at 35,000 feet. One second, everything was business as usual. The next, conversations went quiet, meetings vanished from my schedule, and people looked at me like I had just announced an emergency landing. And yes, I had to wear my own oxygen mask first, not because I couldn't breathe, but because handling the pressure around me suddenly felt like part of the safety drill.

One day I was a fully involved team member. The next, it felt like I had suddenly turned invisible.

Meetings I was always part of suddenly happened without me.

Projects I had led for months were quietly reassigned, without even a handover call.

Coffee break conversations I had been part of turned into polite smiles and quick exits.

I hadn't become incompetent overnight. I had simply become "the one who's leaving."

And that label changed everything.

My manager in particular made it her personal mission to underline my exit at every turn. Until then, I had respected her discipline and precision. But once I resigned, it felt like her respect expired with my notice letter.
Suddenly, every small thing became an issue.

A slightly tired smile after a late night? "You're not setting the right example."

A tiny slip in sequence? "You've been here long enough to know better."

Even when I did things right, recognition vanished. Silence replaced appreciation.

It felt less like feedback and more like judgment. As if my choice to leave meant all my contributions up until then were erased.

My notice period, instead of being a wrap-up, felt like detention. She treated me like a passenger trying to sneak excess baggage onto the plane, eyes narrowed, waiting for me to trip up, ready to call it out.

And then, in the very same company, I experienced the complete opposite.

Another manager, not even my direct boss, took a different approach. She pulled me aside and said softly: "Leaving is part of growth. Don't let this last stretch erase the good you've done. Finish strong, and remember to be proud."

She didn't pile on guilt. She didn't exclude me. She kept me in the loop, asked how I was coping, and even shared her own career stories, times she had to leave roles she loved in order to grow.

She reminded me that my resignation did not cancel out my contribution. She made me feel like my work still mattered, even in those last weeks.

If the first manager clipped my wings, this one helped me stretch them wider.

Two Runways, Two Departures

The contrast couldn't have been clearer.

One manager made me feel like I was sneaking out the back door, guilty for daring to leave.

The other made sure I walked out through the front, head high, suitcase packed, wings intact.
One weighed me down. The other helped me leave with my wings intact.

Beyond the Runway

Leadership is not about how long people stay. It is about how they feel when they leave.

A poor leader treats resignation as betrayal and turns the notice period into punishment. A great leader understands that leaving is part of growth and makes sure the final chapter is one of respect, encouragement, and closure.

Because when someone resigns, you always have a choice.

You can clip their wings with guilt and nitpicking.

Or you can help them grow wings, so they take off stronger, more confident, and grateful for the journey.
One creates bitterness. The other builds alumni.

And the best leaders know this truth: an exit gate is not the end. It is simply another boarding pass. How you handle it decides whether you are remembered as turbulence, or as smooth skies.

Chapter 14:
From Cabin To Classroom

Hanging up the uniform did not mean leaving the skies. It just meant trading the aisle for a classroom. Instead of serving passengers, I was now training future crew and let me tell you, managing a classroom of wide-eyed recruits sometimes felt harder than managing a cabin full of demanding passengers.

On my first day as a trainer, I walked in feeling like I had to be flawless. After all, they were looking at me the way passengers once did, as the calm authority in uniform. But instead of safety demos and meal service, I was teaching grooming standards, CX scripts, and how to smile through turbulence without looking like a nervous wreck.

The funny part? Half the time I learned as much from them as they did from me. A trainee once asked, *"What if a passenger yells at me and I start crying?"* I laughed and said, *"Then you cry later. Right now, you smile and keep serving the tea."* It was not in the manual, but it was honest and honesty made them trust me.

Being a trainer was not about being perfect. It was about showing them that mistakes, nerves, and slip-ups were part of the journey and what mattered was how you recovered.

But this was just the beginning. Aviation training was only a small part of a much bigger vision. I realised these lessons discipline, empathy, people skills, resilience were not just for cabin crew. They applied everywhere: in business, in classrooms, in startups, in life. That realisation eventually shaped **Eduroids**, my education-focused venture.

At Eduroids, aviation-style training was just one chapter. The real mission was broader: to prepare people for the future with a mix of hard skills and people skills. We focused on digital skilling, leadership, AI, and customer experience because no matter how advanced the tools, success still depends on how people connect, collaborate, and communicate.

The cabin was my first classroom. The training room was my second. Eduroids became my third, a flight that was never just about jobs in aviation, but about building confidence and skills for the future of work itself.

Beyond The Runway

Shifting from cabin to classroom taught me that leadership is less about directing and more about shaping.

A good teacher does not just pass on rules. They pass on confidence.

A good leader does not just set targets. They create people who believe they can reach them.

That's the difference between managing and leading.

Managers focus on tasks. Leaders focus on people. One checks if the box is ticked. The other builds someone who can tick boxes long after the leader has gone.

In leadership, training is not a side job. It's the job. Every conversation is a chance to coach. Every mistake is a chance to teach without humiliating. Every success is a chance to remind people, "See, you had it in you all along."

Because when you teach, your influence multiplies. When you mentor, your legacy extends. And when you build others with confidence, they don't just remember the rules, they remember who showed them they were capable in the first place.

The cabin may have been my first classroom. But the classroom was where I really learned what it meant to lead: not by being the loudest voice in the room, but by building voices strong enough to speak without me.

Chapter 15:
The Other Kind Of Turbulence

In the skies, turbulence is bumpy air. On the ground, turbulence looks like a newborn who refuses to sleep and a startup that refuses to stick to the plan.

I thought handling a cabin full of passengers prepared me for anything. Then I became a mother *and* an entrepreneur at the same time. Suddenly my life felt like two flights taking off at once, with me as the crew, the captain, and occasionally the crying passenger too.

On one side was my son, who taught me that no manual, no checklist, and no amount of training could prepare you for a 3 a.m. meltdown. On the other side was my venture, where investors wanted updates, clients wanted results, and everything seemed urgent yesterday. Both cried for attention at the same time- one with actual tears, the other with emails in all caps.

Here's the funny thing: the skills overlapped. Patience, empathy, quick thinking, recovery after mistakes. The same way I soothed a nervous passenger or solved a cabin crisis, I found myself applying to both motherhood and business.

There were nights when I rocked a baby with one arm while replying to an investor with the other.

Days when a sales pitch felt no less nerve-wracking than calming a screaming toddler in public. And moments when I thought, *this is turbulence all over again except there's no seatbelt sign to warn you.*

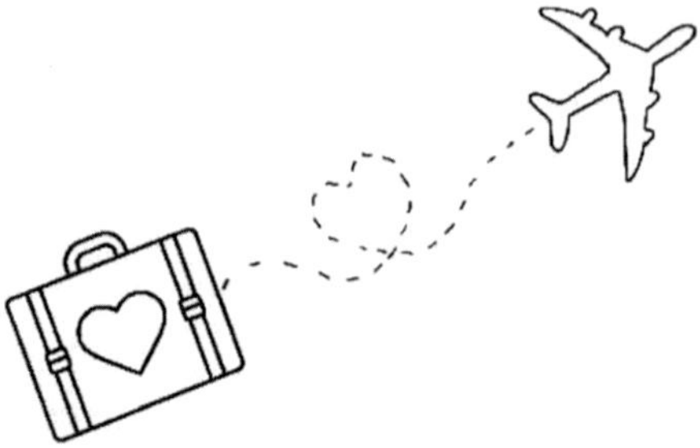

Beyond The Runway

Turbulence on the ground taught me lessons the sky never could.

In life, timing is not always negotiable. Babies arrive when they arrive. Opportunities knock when you least expect them. You don't get to control the schedule. You learn to adapt.

Startups are no different. Plans collapse. Funding shifts. Clients change their minds. Leadership in those moments is not about sticking to the original playbook. It's about rewriting it in real time and keeping people steady while you do it.

Because the truth is, people do not look for leaders to be perfect. They look for leaders to be calm. To say, "We'll figure this out," even when the path is not clear yet.

The cabin taught me how to smile through turbulence. Motherhood and entrepreneurship taught me something deeper: turbulence is not the thing that interrupts the journey. It is the journey. And leadership is learning to walk through it without losing your balance.

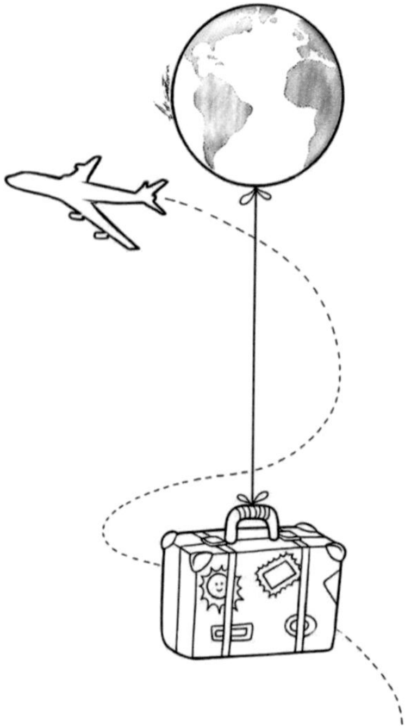

Epilogue – The Final Call

Every journey ends with an announcement. *"Cabin crew, prepare for landing."* Trays up, seatbelts clicked, seat backs upright. The hum of descent begins, a gentle reminder that no matter how high we fly, every flight has a destination.

My own journey has had many take-offs, a few smooth skies, and more turbulence than I ever expected. From the aisle of an aircraft to the front of a classroom. From building a startup to balancing motherhood. From reimagining myself to circling back to the industry that first raised me. I have learned that careers don't move in straight lines. They zigzag. They reroute. Sometimes they stall. Sometimes they soar. And every version of the journey teaches you something new.

Here's the truth: people do not remember the perfect flights. They remember how they felt when things went wrong, and who helped them through it. That is as true in leadership and life as it is in the cabin.

What I have learned is this: calm is not the absence of chaos. Calm is how you carry yourself through it. Whether you are at 35,000 feet, or in a boardroom, or at your kitchen table, leadership is not a title. It's an attitude. It's the way you steady others while finding your own balance.

So, fasten your seatbelt. Take a deep breath. Remember: you are the calm in someone else's chaos. And sometimes, that's the greatest service of all.

And with that, this is your captain speaking for the final time in this book: thank you for flying with me. Until our next journey together - safe travels, steady skies, and happy landings.